04 패턴의 구성
Pattern Components

드레스 패턴
Dress Pattern

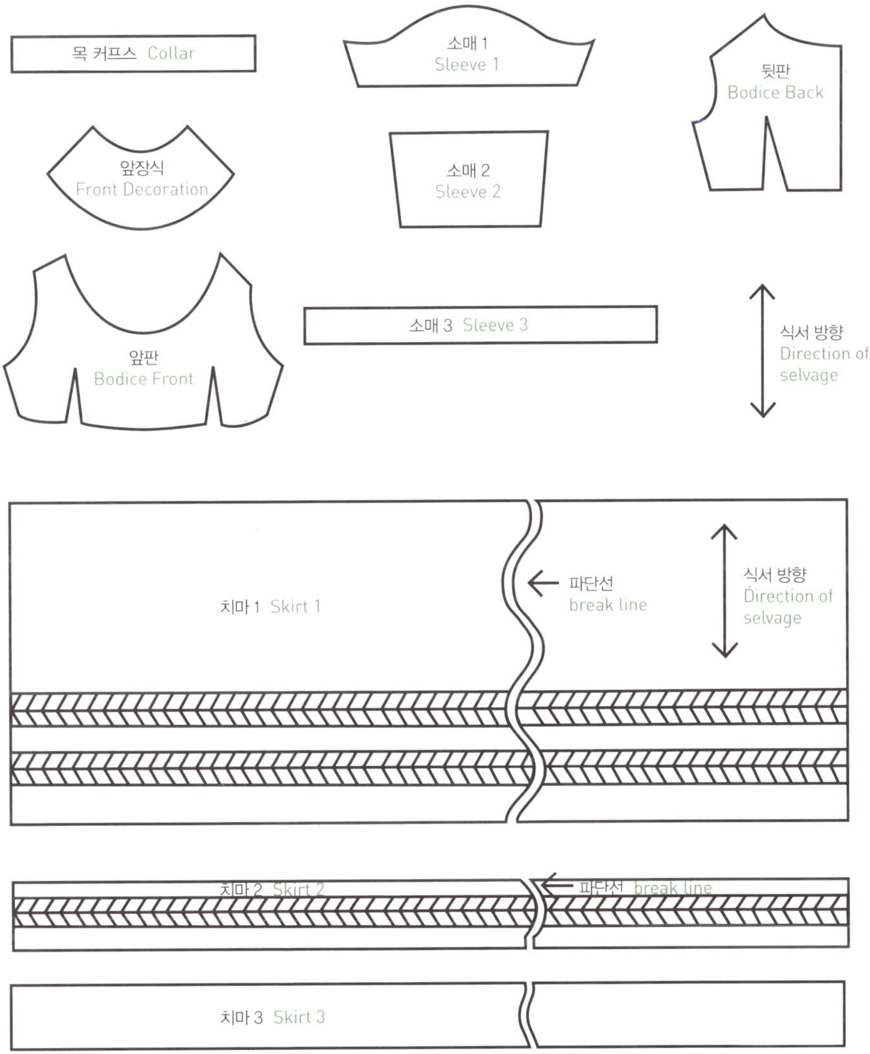

속치마용 패턴
Underskirt Pattern

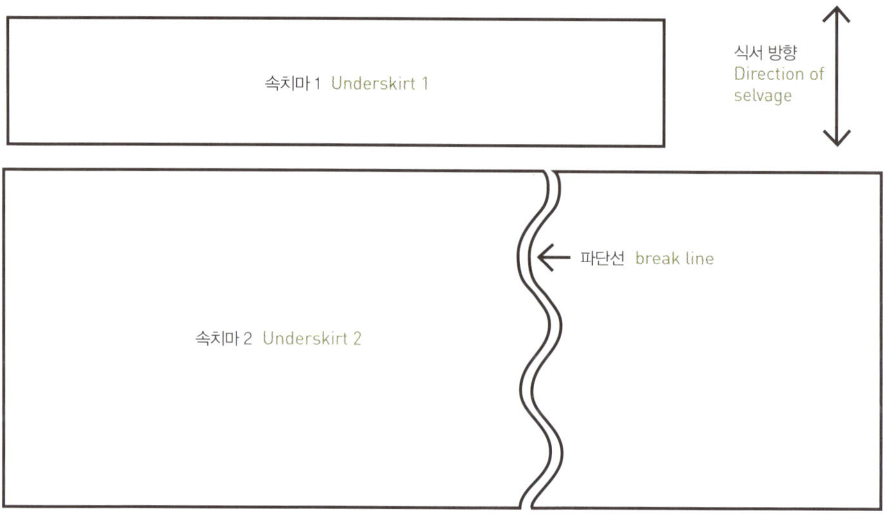

보닛용 패턴
Bonnet Pattern

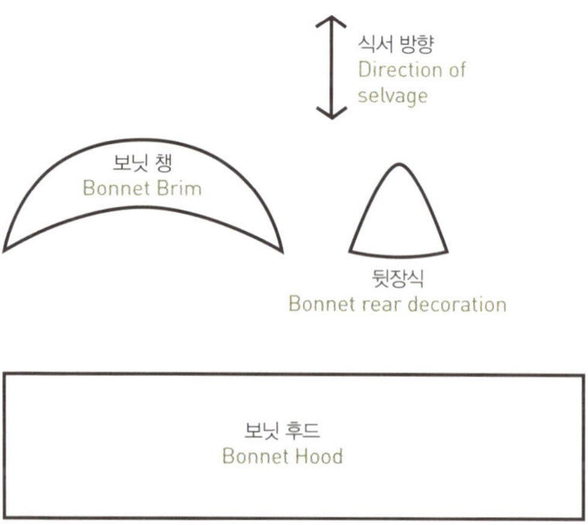

스타킹용 패턴
Stocking Pattern

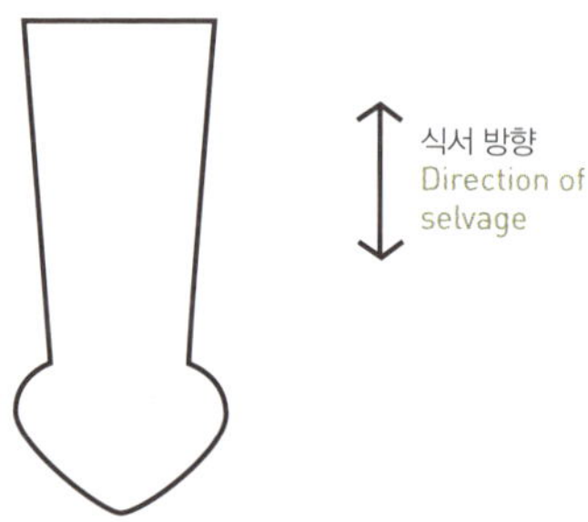

참고) 정확한 패턴 크기는 뒷면의 실물크기를 참조하세요.
Note: For accurate measure, please refer to the full-scale patterns on the other side.

05 드레스만들기 Making the Dress

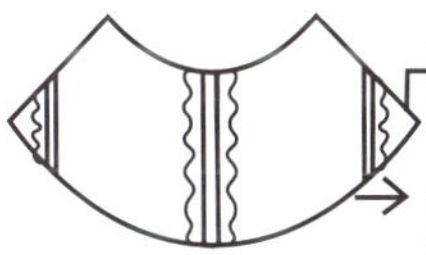

1. 앞 장식에 면레이스를 박고,위에 0.5cm공단 테이프를 눌러 박는다.

1. Sew cotton lace on Front Decoration, and sew ¼" width satin tape, pressing onto the lace.

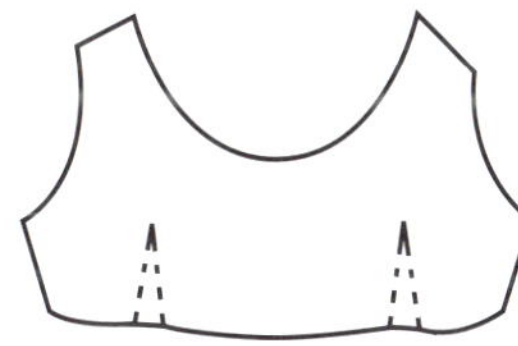

2. 앞판의 다아트 부분을 3.5cm 길이로 눌러 박는다.

2. Press and sew darts 1⅜" long on the Bodice Front.

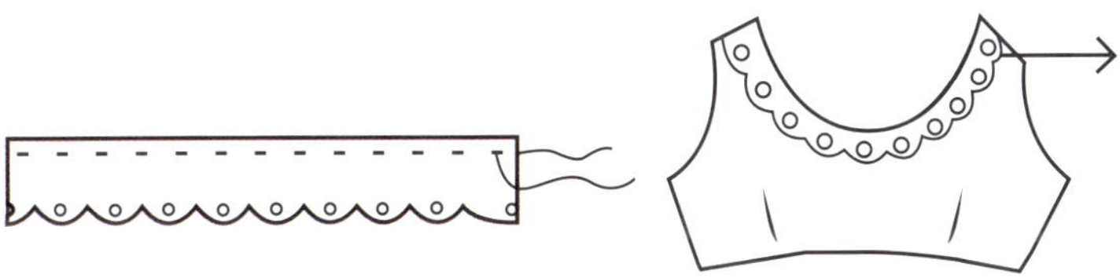

3. 앞판의 앞장식을 달 부분에 면레이스를 주름잡아 박는다. 면레이스의 박음한 실중 하나를 잡아 당기면 자연스럽게 주름이 잡힌다.

3. Pleat cotton lace and sew it onto the Bodice Front. Pull a stitched thread to make it frill naturally.

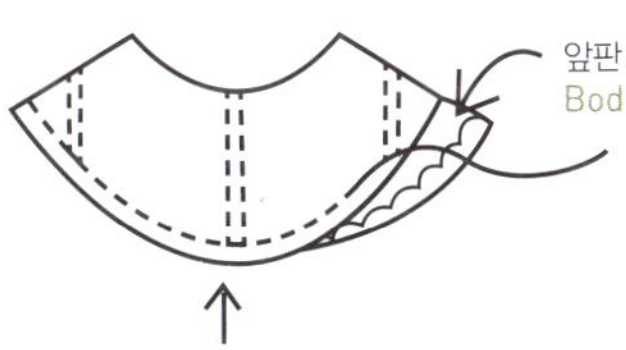

4. 앞장식과 앞판을 자연스럽게 이어주고,겉에서 눌러 박는다. 앞장식의 뒷쪽에서 앞판의 면레이스 부분에 대고 재단선을 따라 자연스럽게 박아준다.

4. Join Front Decoration to Bodice Front, and sew them together, pressing from above. Put the inside of Front Decoration to the cotton lace part of the Bodice Front, and sew them together along the cutting line.

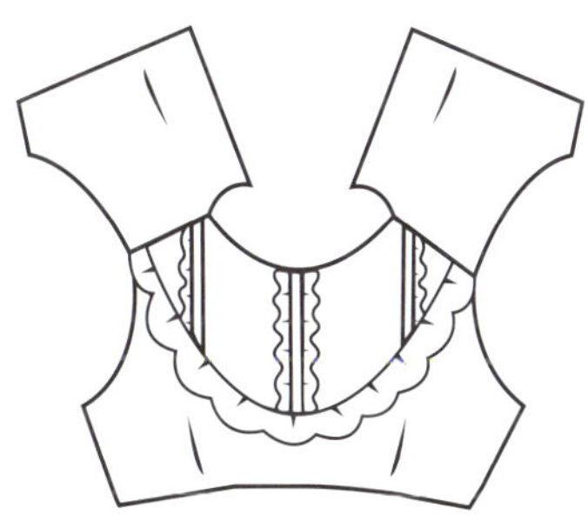

5. 뒷판에 다아트를 넣고 앞판과 뒷판을 연결한다.

5. Sew darts on the Bodice Back, and join it to the Bodice Front.

6. 목커프에 레이스를 달아 눌러박는다.
6. Press and sew Lace onto the Collar.

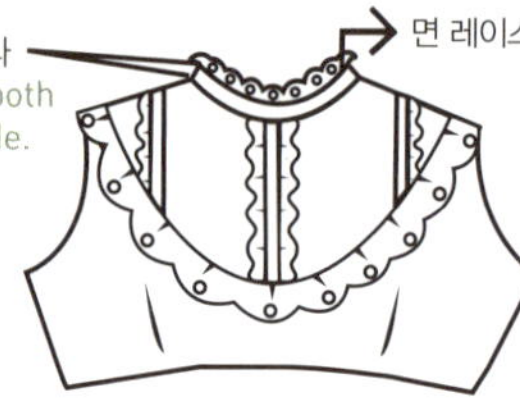

7. 목부분에 커프스를 단다.
7. Sew Collar around the neck line.

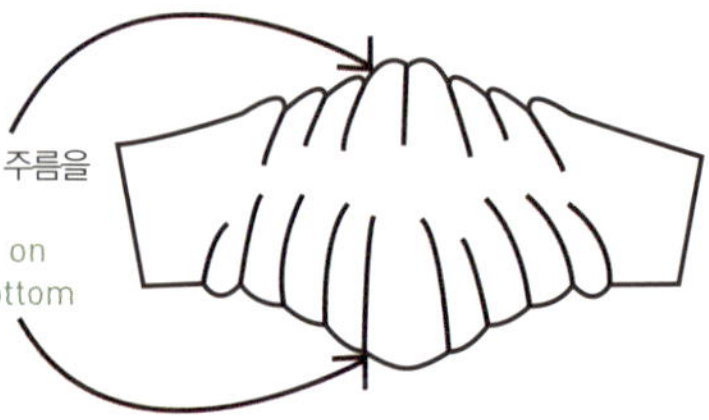

소매①은 위아래 주름을 잡아 놓는다.
Pleat Sleeve 1 on the top and bottom side.

8. 소매①부분은 가운데부분만 주름 잡아 놓고, 소매②는 가운데 부분에 0.5cm공단 테이프를 박고 리본 장식을 해 놓는다. 소매③은 한쪽에 레이스를 달아 놓는다.
8. Pleat Sleeve 1, in the middle only : Sew ¼"- width satin tape on Sleeve 2, along the midway, and attach a ribbon ; Sew lace on Sleeve 3, on one side.

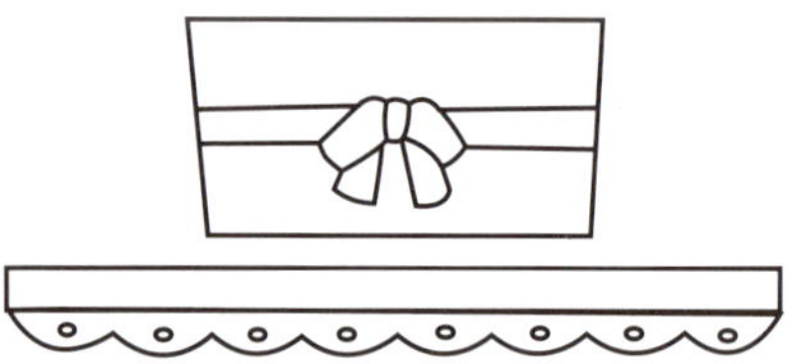

소매②는 공단 테이프를 박고 리본을 접어 가운데를 눌러 박는다.
Sew satin tape on Sleeve 2, tie a ribbon, and sew it, pressing in the middle.

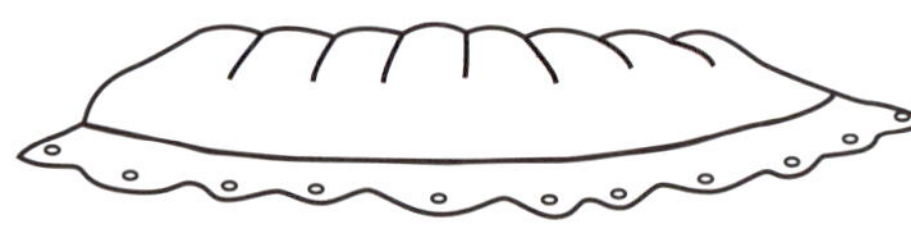

소매③은 레이스를 달아 놓고 윗쪽은 주름잡아 놓는다.
Put lace on Sleeve 3, and pleat the upper part.

9. 소매①,소매②,소매③을 순서대로 박아 소매 2장을 만든다.
9. Put Sleeves 1, 2 and 3 and sew them in the order, making two sleeves.

〈그림〉은 안쪽 모습입니다.
This is the inside view.

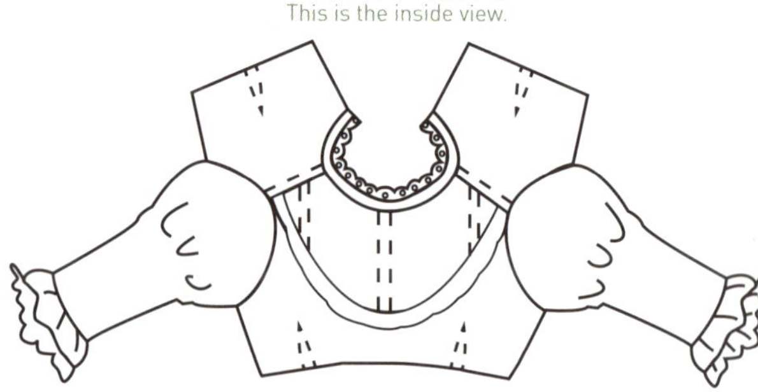

10. 몸쪽에 소매 2장을 단다.
10. Sew the sleeves onto the bodice.

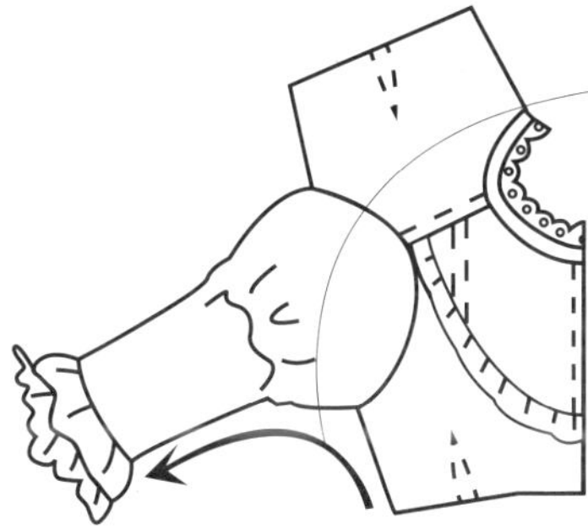

11. 앞판과 뒷판을 연결하면서 겨드랑이를 지나 소매쪽까지 눌러 박는다.

11. Press and sew from bodice through armpit to Sleeve, joining the Front and Back Bodices.

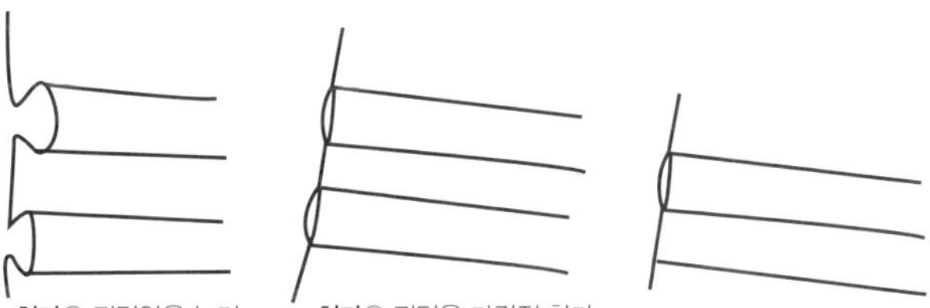

12. 치마①에 핀턱 2줄을 넣고, 치마②에도 핀턱 1줄을 넣어 치마 밑쪽 방향으로 다림질해 놓는다.

12. Make two rows of pin tuck on Skirt 1 : Make one row of pin tuck on Skirt 2, and iron them downward.

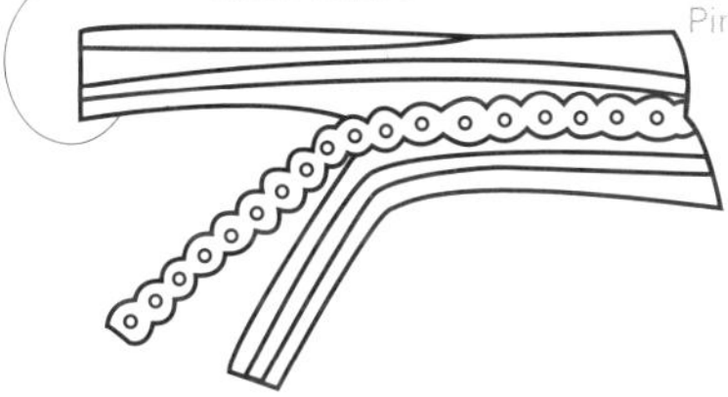

13. 치마①과 치마②사이에 장미 레이스를 단다.

13. Sew Rose Lace between Skirts 1 and 2.

14. 치마③에 레이스 달고 눌러 박아 손으로 주름 잡아 놓는다.

14. Put lace onto Skirt 3: press and sew them, then make pleats by hand.

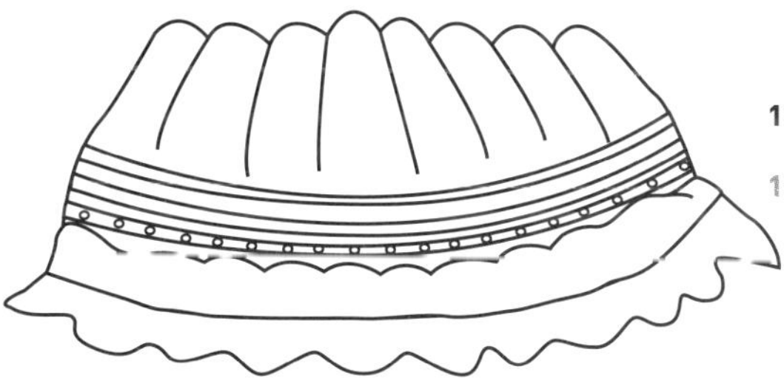

15. 치마①과 치마②,치마③을 연결해 치마①의 상단이 약 20cm가 되도록 주름을 잘게 잡아 놓는다.

15. Put Skirts 1, 2 and 3 together : pleat the top of Skirt 1 into 8" length.

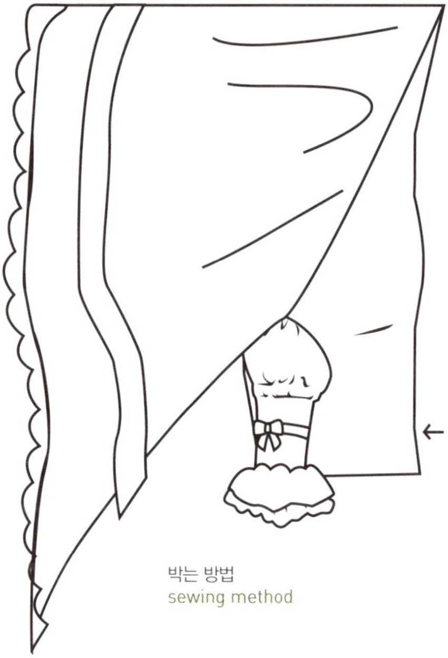

박는 방법
sewing method

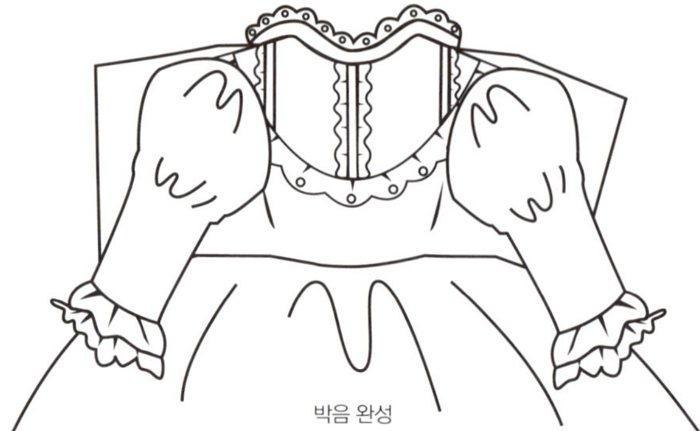

박음 완성
finished view

16. 완성된 드레스 상의 쪽에 치마를 단다.

16. Join the Skirts to the Bodice of the dress.

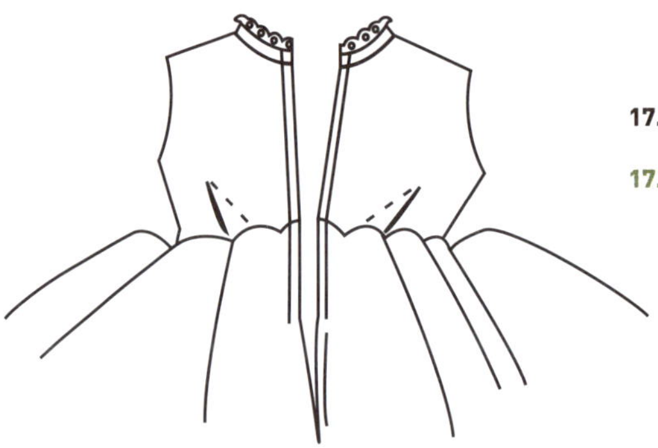

안쪽
inside view

17. 뒷쪽에 콘솔 지퍼를 다림질하여 달아준다. 지퍼달기가 어려우면 똑딱단추를 달아주어도 좋다.

17. Iron the concealed zipper(hidden fastener) and sew it at the back of the dress: or, snaps may do as well.

---

18. 실밥을 정리하여 깨끗하게 마무리 되면 장식용 까메오를 앞쪽 중앙에 꽂아 놓는다.

16. Trim by removing waste threads: decorate with the Cameo by fastening it at the center.

06 속치마 만들기
Making the Underskirt

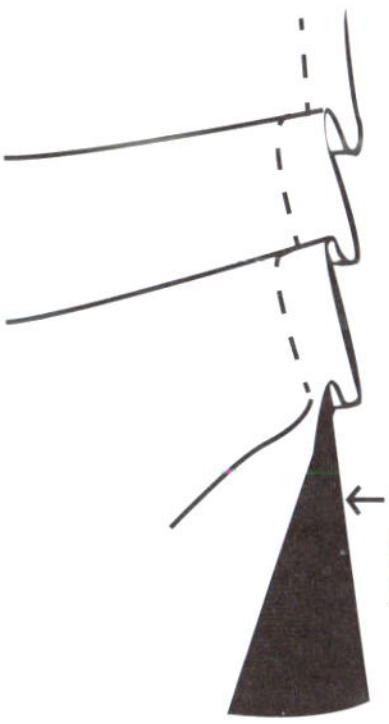

하단부터 상단까지 눌러박아 원으로 만든다.
Press and sew from bottom upward to top, making it cylindrical form.

1. 속치마①에 속치마②(패티코트용 속치마로 재단된 힘있는 원단)를 주름잡으며붙인다.
1. Pleat and join Underskirt 1 and Underskirt 2, which is made with stiff material as a Petticoat.

2. 속치마②에 레이스를 달아준다.
2. Put lace on Underskirt 2.
3. 고무줄을 17cm로 잘라 원으로 만든다.
3. Cut 6¾" of elastic braid connect the ends, making it a ring.
4. 속치마①과 ②를 원으로 박아준다.
4. Join Underskirts 1 and 2, sew them together in a circle.

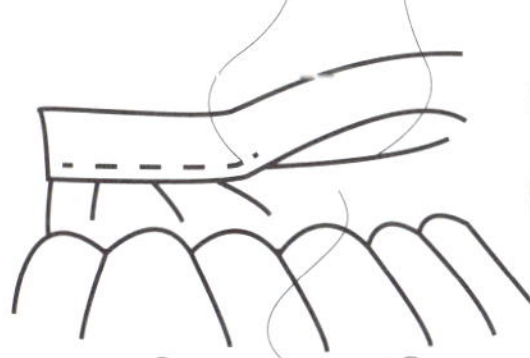

5. 원으로 만들어진 속치마에 원으로 만든 고무줄을 넣으며 박는다.
5. Put the ring-shaped elastic braid at the top of the Underskirt, and sew them together.

---

07 보닛 만들기
Making the Bonnet

레이스를 창의 안쪽으로 향하도록 달아준다.
Put lace facing inner side of the brim.

1. 보닛의 챙부분의 안쪽에 접착심을 다리미로 붙이고 보닛챙 겉쪽에 레이스를 단다.
1. Fix adhesive pad onto inside of the Bonnet Brim with iron: put lace on the outer side of Bonnet Brim.

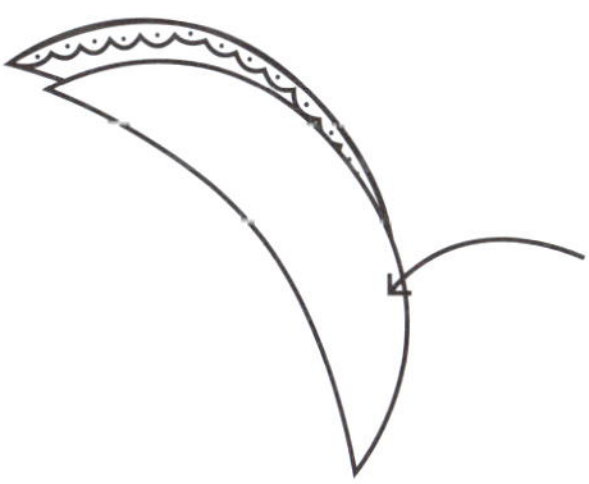

2. 레이스를 단 겉지와 안지를 붙여 뒤집어 눌러 박아준다.
2. Join the inner and outer side brims with the lace in-between: sew the brims together, pressing.

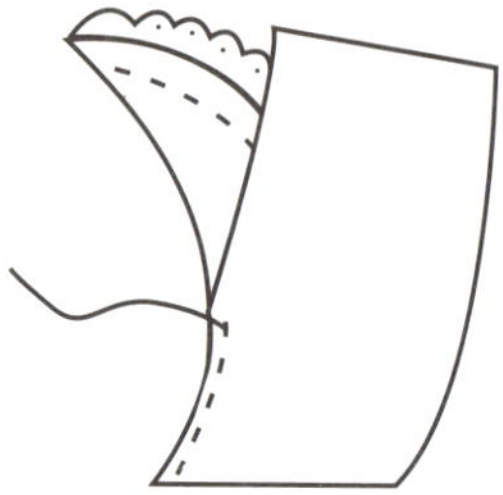

3. 보닛챙에 보닛후드를 달아준다.
3. Stitch Bonnet Hood to Bonnet Brim.

4. 보닛후드에 뒷장식을 주름잡아 달아준다.
4. Pleat Bonnet Rear Decoration: attach it to the Bonnet Hood.

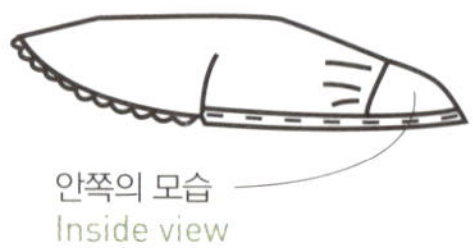

5. 보닛후드와 뒷장식을 보닛챙의 길이에 맞게 접어 박아준다.
5. Adjust Bonnet Hood and Rear Decoration to the length of Brim, and sew them.

6. 보닛에 레이스와 리본 장식을 한 후 검정 공단 테이프 줄을 달아 보닛 여밈줄로 이용할 수 있게 해준다.
6. Decorate Bonnet with lace and ribbon: then fasten black satin strings to be used for tying up.

08 스타킹 만들기
Making the Stockings

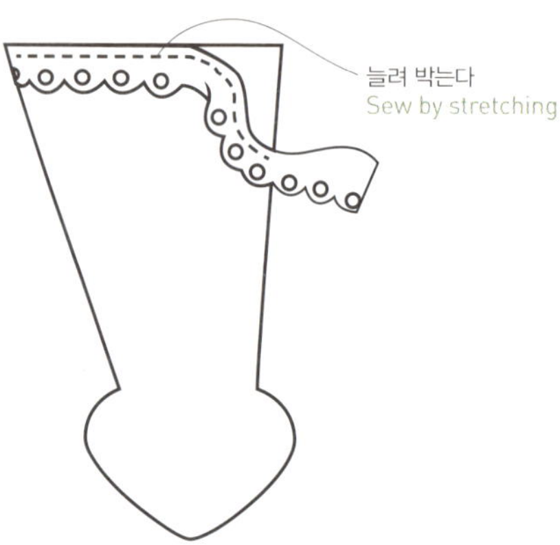

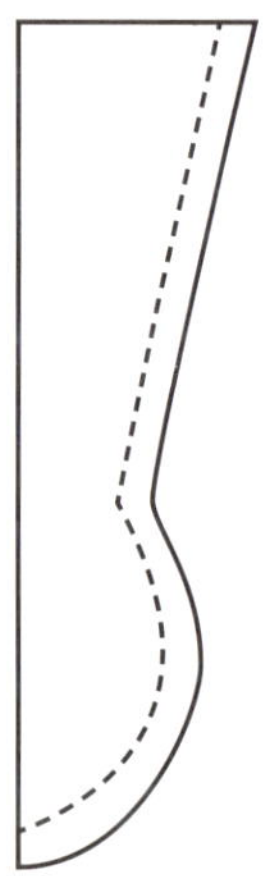

1. 스타킹의 스타킹 윗쪽 재단선에 스판레이스를 늘려 가며 달아, 신고 벗기 편안하게 박아준다.
1. Sew the spandex lace while stretching it along the top line of the stocking, to make it easy to put on.

2. 스타킹을 아래부터 위로 접어서 박아준다.
2. Fold the Stocking and sew from bottom to top.

돌모아의 샤브레 드레스 패턴집을 선택해 주셔서 감사합니다.

돌모아는 2002년 2월 22일 콜렉터블돌 전문 인터넷 쇼핑몰로 탄생하였습니다.
모우고 싶은 콜렉터의 마음을 담은 말로 한글로 모아(모우다)를 발음 나는데로 표현한
이중적인 의미를 가진 합성어 입니다.

돌모아에서는 구체관절인형및 다양한 인형관련제품(가발,신발,의상,안구,돌스탠드,
인형가구,인형악세사리,인형제작에 필요한 다양한 재료등)을
생산 및 판매하고 있습니다.

인형 콜렉터를 위한 세계적인 인형개발사 및 출판사로 거듭날 수 있도록
노력하는 돌모아가 되겠습니다.

주소 서울 송파구 방이동 126-2 2층 돌모아
전화 02-3432-4993(AM10:00~PM 06:00)
http://www.dollmore.com
http://www.dollmore.net
http://www.dollmore.co.kr
email:necking@dollmore.com

파본은 구입처에서 교환해 드립니다.
항상 돌콜렉터의 마음으로 최선을 다하겠습니다.

DOLLMORE
Ball Joint Doll Company

서울 송파구 방이동 126-2 2층 돌모아 | tel 02-3432-4993
http://www.dollmore.com, http://www.dollmore.net,
http://www.dollmore.co.kr | email:help@dollmore.net
copyright©2009 By Dollmore All right reserved

Dollmore's Crafts

DD 01

www.dollmore.com

Making the Chavret Dress

샤브레 드레스 만들기

Model : Dollmore Kid Doll "**paran**"(키 : 43cm)

값 5,500원

ISBN 978-89-961720-2-4

01 재료 Material

❶ 검정 스트라이프 원단 110cm 한마
❷ 면레이스 360cm
❸ 치마 밑단용 테이프 장미레이스 80cm
❹ 0.5cm 공단 테이프 90cm
❺ 0.5cm 공단 테이프 80cm
❻ 모자용 장미 레이스 20cm
❼ 드레스 장식용 까메오 한개
❽ 스타킹용 흰색 스판천 가로20cm×세로15cm
❾ 스타킹용 흰색 스판 레이스 20cm
❿ 속치마용 고무줄 17cm
⓫ 속치마 패티코트용 망사 가로80cm×세로12cm
⓬ 속치마용 공단천 가로40cm×세로5cm
⓭ 콘솔지퍼,접착심 약간

❶ Black stripe fabric of 44" - width : 1 yd or 36".
❷ Cotton lace : 4 yd or 144"
❸ Rose tape lace for the hem : 32"
❹ ¼"- width satin tape : 1 yd or 36"
❺ ¼"- width satin tape: 32"
❻ Rose lace for the hat: 8"
❼ Cameo for decoration: 1 ea.
❽ White spandex for the stockings : 8" width×8" length
❾ White spandex lace for the stockings : 8"
❿ Elastic braid for the underskirt : 6¾"
⓫ Gauze for the petticoat : 32" width×4¾" length
⓬ Satin for the underskirt : 16" width×2" length
⓭ Concealed zipper(hidden fastener), adhesive pad

02 도구 Tools

자, 가위 , 쵸크, 실핀
Ruler, Scissors, Chalk, Pins

03 패턴 Patterns

❶ 드레스용 패턴
❷ 속치마용 패턴
❸ 보닛용 패턴
❹ 스타킹용 패턴

❶ Dress Pattern
❷ Underskirt Pattern
❸ Bonnet Pattern
❹ Stocking Pattern